CROW TAROT

by MJ Cullinane

Copyright © 2019 U.S. Games Systems, Inc.

All rights reserved. The illustrations, cover design, and contents are protected by copyright. No part of this booklet or deck may be reproduced in any form without permission in writing from the publisher, except by a reviewer who wishes to quote brief passages in connection with a review written for inclusion in a magazine, newspaper or website.

20 19 18 17 16 15 14 13 12 11

Made in China

Published by
U.S. GAMES SYSTEMS, INC.
179 Ludlow Street
Stamford, CT 06902 USA
www.usgamesinc.com

*A very special thank you to my
beautiful daughter River who
inspires me every day to create art
for the sake of happiness first.*

CROW TAROT

Fly Through the Veil

Crows have always held a special place in my heart. I cannot pinpoint when or why it started, but for as long as I can remember, since I was a little girl growing up south of Boston, they have fascinated me. It may be because when I look into their eyes, I get a distinct feeling that they know something so much more significant than I could ever comprehend, something other-worldly.

From the perspective of an artist, I often find myself mesmerized by crows' feathers, as each one holds a myriad of colors. When the sunlight washes over their bodies they appear vibrant and iridescent, as shades of purple, deep indigo and soft caramel play in the light. Then, poof—in an instant the bird will turn pitch black as if creating a hole in space before my eyes.

Living in Seattle, crows are a noticeable part of the landscape. From the beach to the mountains, they dot the skies, speckle the sand and top the trees. I am fortunate to have a record number of crows fly through our neighborhood, stopping along the way to pick up a treat or spend an afternoon on the telephone wires cawing at strangers. They serve as an excellent alarm system when something nearby is amiss!

Crow energy is intense and mystical. (In some cultures, they are known as tricksters and shapeshifters, with an ability to morph into other animals or humans.) Crows never forget a face; and if we are open, they let us connect with them in an extraordinary, almost soulful, way. Like humans, crows can hold a grudge for a lifetime; they also pass down stories, to warn future generations of the dangers around them.

Crows are truly remarkable creatures. When I set out to create my first tarot deck, it made sense that I use my favorite muse as the focus. Developing the project, I had two goals. First, to make each card a piece of art that pays homage to crows and ravens. Second, to infuse each image with familiar symbolism from the original Rider-Waite Tarot so that both novice and professional tarot readers would be able to use the deck with confidence, without needing to memorize new interpretations.

I believe we all possess the answers to our life questions, everything we need to know is already within us—we only need to tap into the source. With the use of tarot cards, we have a direct channel to our higher self. When used correctly, tarot cards are less of a fortune-telling novelty than a useful tool for self-discovery.

For daily use, I prefer to pull three cards, rather than just one, asking the deck to tell me a story. I usually find myself contemplating the cards long after the reading. I often discover something new about myself that I had either overlooked or avoided. At other times I find a different way of tackling the problem.

For all those who use this deck, may you connect with the intuitive power of the crow and fly through the veil.

MAJOR ARCANA

THE FOOL

KEYWORDS: Innocence, Beginnings, Free-spirit, Faith, Adventure

ELEMENT: Air

Unafraid, the crow does not waiver a bit and has faith that the log and river will provide a great adventure. In the distance there is a wind blowing, whistling a warning. Yet the crow remains faithful knowing that despite how stormy or choppy the waters may become in the future the log will keep her afloat. The Fool card asks that you have faith in the universe and live fearlessly. You will come through the storm. If you allow hope to replace fear, imagine the adventures you have waiting.

Upright, this card is urging you to have faith. Reversed, this card is asking you to assess whether or not you are pushing belief past its limits. Your higher self is sending you a warning that, although the universe has your back, it is not an open invitation to make foolish or adverse decisions that could have a severe and negative impact on your future.

1. THE MAGICIAN

KEYWORDS: Alchemy, Resourcefulness, Creativeness, Manifesting

ELEMENT: Air

Connecting the physical world with the spiritual realm, the Magician crow pulls the energy of the four suits representing earth, water, air, and fire to create a spark that has the power to manifest into a transformative idea. Rising above the craggy desolate mountains lined by red and white roses at the base, the Magician symbolizes the first steps of generating success. He has the ability to carve out the desired path through difficulty, using life experiences and a pure heart.

Sometimes, however, the crow is an impostor, a trickster. Reversed, the Magician crow uses the connected power of the spiritual realm for greedy purposes. The Magician in this position may denote you have fallen prey and have become another gullible victim. Take the time to look inward and ask if your motives are pure of heart.

2. THE HIGH PRIESTESS

KEYWORDS: Intuition, Spirit guides, Divine guidance, Magick

ELEMENT: Water

The High Priestess takes the spark created by the Magician and transforms the idea into a tangible reality. Like a shadow passing in the night, her energy is present and can be felt in the gut, but not always seen. Her intuitive power lies in the spiritual unconscious, allowing the High Priestess to soar back and forth through the veil bringing with her divine knowledge. Perched on the moon and surrounded by the four suits, your connection with the High Priestess is active at this time and should be utilized. She comes ready to deliver the answers you seek through dreams and symbols. Pay attention; she is with you.

If the High Priestess appears reversed, it is a message that your connection with your inner-self has been lost. As a result, the High Priestess is unable to communicate the information you need to make a wise decision. She strongly urges you to take time for yourself and to allow for communication to come to you through the quietness of spirit. Her message is to pay attention; there is magic in this world, you only need to allow yourself to experience it.

3. THE EMPRESS

KEYWORDS: Motherhood, Abundance, Business success, Creativity

ELEMENT: Earth

The fertile Empress flies over the abundant lush landscape of Mother Earth. She is uplifted by the warmth that radiates from her connectedness with the planet. The Empress sends a loving message to take time to pamper yourself and to embrace the feminine energy within all of us. Her spirit is pure love and bringing things to life; she asks that you go into nature to feel the soothing and healing power that invigorates the soul. When the Empress pays a visit, she may bring a message of a new birth.

Reversed, the Empress is a warning that

the lack of harmony you are feeling is a result of being disconnected from your friends or family, or from nature. Your heart is shielded, making building relationships difficult. The Empress is calling out to you asking that you go inward and be creative. Only when you accept yourself and direct your heart's loving energy inward, will you be free to radiate love and compassion outward to others.

4. THE EMPEROR

KEYWORDS: Father-like, Authority, Fair-minded, Wisdom, Protective

ELEMENT: Fire

The Emperor represents masculine father energy. Whereas the Empress offers abundant love and nurturing, the Emperor brings a solid foundation of order and rules that provide security and stability. The crow stands on a sword, a symbol of power, protection, authority, strength and courage. The ram head on the throne represents leadership and initiative. The Emperor's energy brings order to chaos. He is not a dictator nor taskmaster; he is, however, a strong leader who commands devotion through wisdom and integrity. Crows are known for passing information through their DNA to future generations to protect them from possible dangers. The Emperor sits on his throne ready to share his knowledge to ensure all around him stay safe. Channel his power in times of uncertainty. Through fearless determination and expertise it will manifest success.

If the Emperor appears reversed, this may serve as a warning that arrogance and over-confidence are getting in the way. As a result, you risk losing the respect you crave.

5. THE HIEROPHANT

KEYWORDS: Education, Tradition, Religious institutions, Higher learning

ELEMENT: Earth

The Hierophant crow is pragmatic and does not take unnecessary risks. This crow appears at a time when a conventional approach is needed to resolve a situation or help further a project. This card brings a warning that now is not a time to think outside the box. Instead, seek knowledge from a well-regarded institution or person. The Hierophant's role is to stand before others as a mentor and spiritual teacher. He is deeply connected with the divine and could represent guidance that comes from connecting with our higher self through a professional healer.

When the Hierophant appears reversed, it may imply a need to be less restrictive in your thought process and creative thinking.

6. THE LOVERS

KEYWORDS: Love, Business partnership, Choices, Relationships

ELEMENT: Air

On the surface this card represents love and unity. However, it goes deeper as it also describes karmic passion and soul relationships that span lifetimes. The crows have traveled together through space and time. Drinking from the same heart binds them as their veins fill with the same life force, joining their spirit for eternity. Together, each decision is made as the outcome will forever affect them both. From the person you love to the place you settle down, this card asks that you examine your belief system and use your inner compass when deciding to join forces. The Lovers brings the message that some benefits and consequences will eventually reveal themselves for better or for worse.

The Lovers reversed may tell of an imbalance in a relationship. As a result, you may discover you are not being honest with yourself about the reasoning behind your decision. Take the time to check in, meditate, and examine your choices.

7. THE CHARIOT

KEYWORDS: Determination, Willpower, Drive, Success

ELEMENT: Water

The triumphant crow, soaring through the stormy sky with fearlessness and strength, rides a chariot of thunderous clouds to victory. The Chariot is a sign to go forward with confidence, knowing that your well-executed plan will be a success. It asks that you summon your power to fly above the barriers and soar through obstacles. The crow who rides victoriously on the chariot has learned to harness his aggression, extracting only the positive energy required to finish the task.

In contrast, the reversed Chariot could indicate a loss of control or being dragged into a situation that may not lead to the best outcome.

8. STRENGTH

KEYWORDS: Inner strength, Passion, Virility, Confidence

ELEMENT: Fire

It is not through brute force that this crow has achieved the challenging goal of taming the wild beast; it is because she has mastered her ability to connect with a higher-frequency, channeling trust and respect. The positive energy she radiates enables the crow to balance confidently on the lion's nose, not in conquest but out of mutual respect. The crow has learned how to remove her ego, quieting the hum of fear, allowing her to hear the inner guidance of her higher conscious. It is from this place she wields the true power of strength. The Strength card suggests you will have an experience that requires you to summon the power that comes only from exercising inner peace and freeing yourself from the influences of ego and fear.

When reversed, Strength may be warning that you are not in control of your emotions and that your motives are fear or ego based. Ask yourself if your strength comes from power or force.

9. THE HERMIT

KEYWORDS: Meditation, Time alone, Enlightenment, Wisdom

ELEMENT: Earth

The solitary hermit crow, aged and wise, is perched upon a sacred tree in quiet contemplation deep in the woods. He listens to what the tree needs to say as the falling snow lands on the smallest of branches. It is the tree that has provided the crow knowledge and is a symbol of the subconscious mind. After his time of quiet reflection, he is ready to pass his knowledge to those who are willing and prepared to travel into the thickest part of the woods. In his mouth, he holds a lantern, a symbol of wisdom to light the way. The soft, bright glistening snowflakes represent cleansing and moving in a spiritual direction that will lead to fulfillment on one's journey.

The reversed Hermit suggests that you have retreated not for self-discovery, but instead to escape day-to-day challenges that have left you feeling overwhelmed. Spending too much time alone may lead to feeling isolated or self-absorbed. Ask yourself if you are recharging or retreating.

10. WHEEL OF FORTUNE

KEYWORDS: Cycle of life, Ups and downs, Luck

ELEMENT: Fire

What goes around comes around and so does the Wheel of Fortune. During difficult times, this card serves as a reminder that with the bad comes the good and a change is coming. The three crows in the center point inward, symbolizing our inner power to move the wheel and our ability to control the amount of time we spend either "up" or "down." The eight crows facing outward on the wheel represent the spokes of the wheel and the energy that each direction possesses. Although they appear to be fixed to the wheel, their wings allow them some freedom, symbolizing our ability to learn from and move past a difficult situation.

Upright, this card indicates that change is coming, and it will be a welcome shift. Perhaps a difficult time is ending. Reversed, however, it is a warning that difficult times will soon come. How quickly you can make the wheel spin is up to you. The question to ask yourself now is—are these troubles a result of bad luck or bad choices?

11. JUSTICE

KEYWORDS: Fairness, Balance, Law

ELEMENT: Air

The crow flies upward with wings open; he has nothing to conceal. His honesty has earned him the respect of his peers as they know he will take a balanced and fair approach to every situation. This crow of Justice brings the message to take the time to see a problem or difficult challenge from all sides before making any decisions. It is also time to consider all consequences.

If Justice is reversed, it may indicate that there is a person who hasn't been completely honest. If you look deep inside, that person may even be yourself. It may be a good time to examine your personal truths.

12. THE HANGED MAN

KEYWORDS: Delay, Letting go, Waiting, Waiting to decide

ELEMENT: Water

The crow hangs from the blossoming cherry tree allowing his wings to fall in complete surrender. He stays still, leaning into the position and allowing the blood to rush in to nourish his brain. Away from the raucous noises of the roost, he has let go and is at peace. It is in the silence he will discover the answers he needs to help move a project or desire forward. The Hanged Man asks that you put the situation or plan on pause so that you can look at it from a different angle. There may be a vital element that you are missing, and the result may be a longer delay. The Hanged Man may suggest getting away from the situation both mentally and physically so that you can recharge your energy and approach the issue with a renewed vitality. This card may also represent a project put on hold due to an external force out of your control. The only course of action is to wait patiently.

In contrast, the reversed Hanged Man feels as though he has been putting in too much effort compared to the amount of success he is seeing. It may also point to a person who has lost faith in his or her idea and is ready to give up without doing the necessary spiritual work that would help in finding a solution.

13. DEATH

KEYWORDS: Change, Ending, New beginning, Transformation, Mortality

ELEMENT: Water

The crow has let go and made peace with the change that must take place for her life to move forward in a positive direction. Her death is symbolic of transformation and comes with a warning. Unless you are willing to sacrifice the part of you that is holding you back, you will feel pain or discomfort in the future. This card marks a profound change coming, one that has the possibility of creating a positive outcome, if you can allow the change to happen without fear of the unknown.

Death reversed is a sign that you are resisting change and holding on to behaviors or thought patterns that are preventing your growth. Take this as a warning to look at the habits that are preventing you from reaching your full potential.

14. TEMPERANCE

KEYWORDS: Moderation, Alchemy, Angel communication

ELEMENT: Fire

The energy of this crow is patient and balanced. She has the power to project grace and calm on the outside while actively solving problems and figuring out solutions to complicated issues inside. When the Temperance card appears, it is a sign to take a long-term view when embarking on a journey or seeking a solution.

Just as the crow blends two opposite liquids, try to blend and harmonize with the people around you. When working with others, ask for their input and incorporate their ideas—perhaps something totally new will come of it.

When reversed, Temperance warns of being shortsighted and feeling a lack of balance or harmony in your day-to-day life. Temperance is about moderation. If you find yourself feeling overly emotional about a situation, seek ways to balance your energy.

15. THE DEVIL

KEYWORDS: Addiction, Bondage, Temptation, Violence

ELEMENT: Earth

Perched in the middle of a river of blood atop his latest prey, the Devil is disinterested in the lives he has destroyed. His presence can be cold and dark. At times, to catch his prey, he channels his charming nature and allows the unsuspecting victim to willingly follow, only to discover later he has taken their joy and replaced it with despair. Chained, yet able to free herself if she sincerely wishes, is a little bird symbolizing purity and a free spirit that has succumbed to the forceful demands of the Devil. This card can mean that there is an addiction that is preventing you from finding real freedom and happiness. It may also indicate a fear of change. This card points out that the chains that have you bound may be of your own creation.

The Devil reversed is a sign that you are no longer blinded by the materialism and over-indulgences of the Devil. You can free your mind and body from the shackles that have kept you from realizing your real potential.

16. THE TOWER

KEYWORDS: Drastic change, Upheaval, Catastrophe

ELEMENT: Fire

Each night the crows gather to roost in the top of an old bell tower that sits on a hill, away from the city lights. The tower has always provided a comfortable shelter that offered security for young and old. That is, of course, until it didn't. The Tower comes with a warning, do not become too comfortable or complacent. Do not think for a moment that it all can't be whisked away in a flash. Mentally prepare yourself; change is always afoot. Sometimes change happens and goes by virtually unnoticed, but not this time. You will feel it, and it will shake your ground. How you manage this change will have a direct impact on how you fare in the future. The energy caused by this change may spark something within that will move you toward a better place. How the pieces fall are up to you.

Change is inevitable, and when the Tower appears reversed, it is a sign that you are doing everything in your power to prevent the necessary course of action. In doing so you are delaying the experience you need to learn from to move forward.

17. THE STAR

KEYWORDS: Wishes, Happiness, Astronomy, Optimism

ELEMENT: Air

Bathing in the crystal clear night sky, the crow allows the water to wash over her wings and cleanse away the negativity of the past. On a branch, a songbird serenades the crow and harkens a time of newfound optimism. The Star card brings the gift of hope and a message that any problematic time in your life will soon be over and the place you find yourself will be one of love and stability. You will feel a profound transformation, one that connects spiritually and as a result, can lead to a lifetime change.

When the Star is reversed, hope and

encouragement are replaced with a feeling of despair and lack of motivation. Take this as a message to quiet your mind and ask yourself what is holding you back? Listen to your gut; it will provide you with the solution to find success and happiness.

18. THE MOON

KEYWORDS: Dreams and nightmares, the Shadow-self, Subconscious, Deception

ELEMENT: Water

In a dream-like state, the crow rests on a branch staring at the moon as it reflects a darker image of herself, her dark side. Below the crow, there is a pond, which represents the subconscious mind with a caged raven symbolizing her wild side that she attempts to restrain. It is the part of herself that she tries to conceal because it evokes feelings of shame. The Moon illuminates areas where we project our insecurities. In doing so, we fall victim to our own harmful powers that may have infiltrated the psyche. Sit by the light of the moon and travel inward to find areas where fear and anxiety have taken control.

The Moon asks, what are you concealing? Learning to recognize and accept all the parts of our being, even the components that may be considered weaknesses, is essential for being whole.

The Moon reversed could signal a time where you release yourself from the bondage of fear and see your life in a brighter, more positive light. It may also suggest a time of heightened psychic abilities.

19. THE SUN

KEYWORDS: Optimism, Positivity, Success, Happiness, Good fortune

ELEMENT: Fire

The crow stands fearlessly on the back of a glistening white horse with her wings reaching outward in freedom. She is open to the radiant energy of the sun as it illuminates her soul and brings success to all she desires to accomplish. She comes to you with the message that luck is on your side and you will soon feel the brightness and warmth of the sun. Bask in all the potential entering into your life at this time and allow this energy to raise your frequency.

If reversed, this card is a sign that you are not able to feel the gifts the Sun has to offer and as a result, there is a feeling of pessimism that is preventing your success. Even if blocked by clouds, the energy of the sun is always there for you. The question is, can you look beyond the clouds to see it?

20. JUDGMENT

KEYWORDS: Transition, Reincarnation, Rebirth

ELEMENT: Fire

The crow calls out for those who are ready to rise up and face their past by accepting the judgment. Only by acknowledging the history will you be able to move forward into the future. Now is an excellent time to meditate and listen to your inner voice. It is only through quiet contemplation that you find a path to absolution. The Judgment card may reflect a recent awakening that has moved you to take stock of any habits or life choices that are holding you back.

When Judgment is reversed, it may suggest that you are not the one in control of your decisions, or that you have given up power. It may also point to a time of being over-judgmental, and as a result, you are missing an opportunity.

21. THE WORLD

KEYWORDS: Successful completions, End of a journey, Wholeness

ELEMENT: Earth

Dancing within a laurel wreath, the crow celebrates. She is surrounded by the four fixed signs: Taurus, Leo, Scorpio and Aquarius, symbolizing the four seasons that mark the passage of time. The World is the last card of the Major Arcana and represents the successful and fruitful end of a journey, one that you have charted since your very first step. The World symbolizes a time of great joy and relief because the hard work you have invested has finally paid off. It is time to revel in the glory of a job well done.

Reversed, this card could indicate you are trying to finish a project, however you may have lost sight of the original vision and are now stuck trying to figure out the next step. You may also have experienced a break in a relationship without the closure needed to move on. Take the time to look inward as your internal compass will point you in the right direction and help the world right itself once again.

MINOR ARCANA

THE SUIT OF WANDS

KEYWORDS:
Intuition, Creativity, Action

ELEMENT: Fire

KING OF WANDS

The King of Wands is an entrepreneurial bird who can take a concept and fly with it. Under the supervision of the King, the idea transforms into reality and will reach its highest potential possible. He is relentless in his pursuit of perfection and with laser-like vision, focuses on the goal. He is a charismatic and natural born leader, although at times he can be a bit arrogant. In a reading, the energy of the King of Wands represents either yourself or someone who has a clear vision of what needs to be accomplished for a project to be successful. Take this as a confirmation that focused energy will result in a positive and fruitful outcome.

The King of Wands reversed may serve as a warning that you are being manipulative or ruthless when it comes to business affairs. It also may be an indication that your hasty decision-making will negatively impact your plans.

QUEEN OF WANDS

The Queen of Wands is a dominant creature sitting on her throne of lions. No one would accuse this bird of being demure. With a plan ready for success, the Queen of Wands often appears as bold, fearless and determined. The Queen appreciates the potential each journey offers and takes the opportunity to learn something new about herself with every challenge. The energy of the Queen of Wands is healthy and agile as she moves through the world with a vibrant flare. With a taste for the best, this is one crow you won't find near the garbage cans as she uses her creative, quick-witted mind to discern the finer things in life.

When this card appears reversed, it is a sign that the Queen of Wands is lacking confidence and feeling scared that she will never live up to the potential she once felt was possible. She urges you to look deep within and ask yourself if fear is holding you back.

KNIGHT OF WANDS

The Knight of Wands channels the charging energy of his horse and moves forward with raw power and determination. With the sun high in the sky offering plenty of daylight ahead, the crow flies without hesitation. He is confident of success, even if he experiences moments of uncertainty about where he is going. The Knight of Wands reflects a person who jumps in without weighing all the consequences. He possesses an energy that is pure enthusiasm, a much-needed ingredient when executing a plan. This card warns that although passion is essential, you must find balance and clear thinking for a project or situation to find success.

Reversed, the Knight of Wands serves as a warning to look out for someone who is impatient to a fault. He too often overlooks important information, and as a result, many of his plans end in failure.

PAGE OF WANDS

The Page of Wands is a messenger of good news. She brings ideas and a creative outlook on life that illuminates any room. Her vibrant, youthful energy is powerful enough to spark a change in direction or push an original project forward. She loves adventure, and although she is ready to travel anywhere her wings will take her, she is not reckless. The Page brings her free-spirited energy to the situation and is prepared to take in all the world has to offer.

When the Page of Wands appears reversed, it may indicate a project that is stuck or can't get off the ground because of unforeseen complications. You may simply have lost interest. Upright, the Page of Wands represents a kind-hearted person. Reversed, the Page of Wands may enter your life as an aggressive, immature bully.

TEN OF WANDS

From a distance, the Ten of Wands didn't appear so big to the crow. However, once committed to carrying the wands, the crow quickly questioned whether or not it made the right choice and if it is now unable to manage the task. Was the treasure worth the effort? This card is a message of caution; you may have taken on responsibilities that could prove to be a bigger burden than anticipated. The Ten of Wands also may reflect an inner strength that will assist you during a time of struggle.

Reversed, the Ten of Wands is a reminder that putting off smaller tasks can lead to a more significant burden.

NINE OF WANDS

After much effort, a final task is almost complete. The Nine of Wands denotes a struggle in finishing a project, and despite the consistent successes of the past, there is one last obstacle that needs to be accomplished before moving forward. The Nine of Wands offers encouragement to keep going! Take a moment to bask in all that you have already created. It is from this place you will find the motivation to continue. You are close to the end; this is not the time to give up after working so hard. Replace the negative feeling or resentment with an open mind and visualize a successful completion.

When reversed, the Nine of Wands cautions against blaming others for your lack of progress and asks you to look inward. Are the obstacles in your way there to teach you a lesson or to self-sabotage because you are fearful of committing fully to the idea or project?

EIGHT OF WANDS

The crow flies swiftly through the air on currents of energy brought by the eight wands. This card brings with it a vitality of spirit. Do not hesitate; now is the time to act. The power of this card is vibrant and expansive. A narrow focus will not serve you at this time; you need to be able to see the big picture. Because the energy is moving quickly, the message of the Eight of Wands is that it is essential to ensure that every task is complete before moving on to the next item on your to-do list.

In contrast, when reversed, the clear path becomes muddled. There may be outside influences or delays, or it may be that you are trying to manifest every idea that pops into your head. If you are feeling overwhelmed, take the time to meditate on what it is you truly want to focus your energy on.

SEVEN OF WANDS

The crow tries to defend his territory at the top of the mountain. The approaching crows below are all too eager to knock him down and take his spot. This card is a reminder that although you've made it, you must not be complacent as there will be those who believe your position should be theirs. The Seven of Wands asks that you remain self-confident and have courage when facing challenges. It won't always be easy at the top, but you've earned the right to be there.

Reversed, the Seven of Wands could indicate a time of lost confidence and feeling too weakened to defend yourself. You may find yourself backing down just to avoid conflict. Take this as an opportunity to rediscover your self-confidence and build your self-esteem.

SIX OF WANDS

High atop a ladder of six wands, perched in the center of a laurel wreath, the crow bathes in the light of the sun symbolizing victory. The flock of crows below offers their respect and admiration. This crow comes to you as an acknowledgment of your hard work and brings an encouraging message. Not only will you find success in your future endeavors, you will also garner the respect and admiration of others.

Reversed, the Six of Wands comes with a warning that your project will not be as successful as you imagined. He may also signal a situation that could risk your reputation with peers. Of course, these are merely warnings; your actions will decide the outcome. The Six of Wands reversed asks you if you might be getting in your own way.

FIVE OF WANDS

Five crows spar in the sky. Each crow brings with it a different color wand, symbolizing diverse histories, philosophies and backgrounds. Although on the surface the conflict may look violent, the crows are competing in a cordial manner and not battling to the death. This card suggests that out of a friendly debate a good amount of progress moves a project forward. The Five of Wands may denote a meeting that brings various groups together to solve a single problem.

Reversed, the Five of Wands indicates a person who is afraid of conflict, and avoids engaging in any form of disagreement, even if it may lead to something positive.

FOUR OF WANDS

Two crows harmoniously chatter as they celebrate the end of another beautiful day. The Four of Wands denotes a time of peace and harmony, especially regarding home and family. The Four of Wands also predicts that a joyous occasion such as a birth or wedding could be on the horizon. You may also see the Four of Wands as a reminder to connect with those who bring joy and happiness into your life. Throw a dinner party, arrange for a backyard barbeque, or have friends over. It may not feel like it at this moment, but you will soon have a reason to celebrate.

When reversed, the Four of Wands represents instability in your home life or a breakdown in a relationship. Although you know that the change is vital to your growth in the long run, you may be finding it difficult to keep a positive attitude.

THREE OF WANDS

Eager for a new adventure, the crow looks across an expansive body of water off in the distance where it sees a new land to explore. He is ready to move beyond the familiar comforts of home to seek new ventures and experiences. The Three of Wands suggests looking for a new beginning or opportunity in your life, whether it is traveling abroad, starting a new project, or going back to school. This card brings the message that now is the time to go after your dreams. They may be significant and as vast as an ocean. Move forward with faith; you will make it across.

Reversed, the Three of Wands indicates a setback. Although the plan was well executed in your head, in reality, there is an unforeseen snag or a patch of bad luck holding you back. It may also be a sign that your heart isn't in the journey.

TWO OF WANDS

The crows holding the wands do so with patience and balance. It takes skill and strength to maintain the world. When the wands come together, they create a spark that sets an idea in motion, one that has the power to create a path to success. These birds bring opportunities for travel as well as the need to make life-changing decisions. Each journey offers the possibility of a new experience. The Two of Wands urges you to get out of your comfort zone because destiny is waiting.

The Two of Wands reversed is a message to look for areas in your life where you are reluctant to make a decision or cannot prioritize your goals.

ACE OF WANDS

The crow swoops from the sky and lands upon a wand marking the beginning of a path to a bright shiny city in the distance. This card affirms that the crow is on the right road and opportunities for success are laid out before her. The blooming spring flowers represent a fresh start. Floating through the air are little white feathers bringing the message that the Ace of Wands represents a new beginning that is divinely guided.

Reversed, the Ace of Wands can indicate there is a roadblock getting in your way. It is an excellent time to reflect on whether your journey is off track because of an external issue, for example too many responsibilities, or if the problem is internal, such as a lack of genuine desire.

THE SUIT OF CUPS

KEYWORDS:
Psychic, Creative, Love, Dreams, Feeling

ELEMENT: Water

KING OF CUPS

The King of Cups is a Zen master who has complete control over his emotions. This regal bird can handle the most tumultuous of situations with grace and compassion. When you receive a royal visit from the King of Cups, it may be a signal to take some quiet time to reflect on the emotions around the situation. What emotional triggers seem to pop up regularly that hold back progress?

When the King of Cups appears reversed, he has transformed into an emotional vampire. The King in this position may indicate you are being manipulated or that you are using emotions as a means of blackmail. This card asks you to take time to examine how your feelings and interactions affect the situation.

QUEEN OF CUPS

On her throne surrounded by the ocean's bounty, the serene queen stares out into the water where she connects with her subconscious mind and receives messages from her higher self. The cup in front of her is covered with feathers and represents her inner thoughts. The Queen of Cups denotes loving, intuitive energy that may be found in an older woman in your life during a time that you seek healing. This energy may also manifest in yourself during times you need self-love. The Queen of Cups brings a gift of compassion and emotional connectedness that may be directed toward you or that you will direct to another in need.

The reversed Queen of Cups is someone who is trapped by her feelings. She has learned to suppress her feelings, so as not to become too emotional. As a result, she may feel disconnected.

KNIGHT OF CUPS

The Knight of Cups is a calm, healthy, regal crow. He does not charge alongside his horse but instead has mastered the skill of harnessing the energy needed to deliver his message calmly. The flowers that decorate his horse and the fish that make a pattern in the sky symbolize the Knight's gifts of creativity and intuition. He is a dreamy bird who can quickly sweep you off your feet. However, there is a tendency for this knight in shining armor to get wrapped up in dreams. He is often unable to follow through with his plans. The Knight of Cups may enter your life as a creative thinker who will help you with a project. He may appear in your dreams or thoughts as ideas that "pop" in your head. Pay attention to the message this royal messenger delivers.

When reversed, the Knight of Cups may represent a person who has become overly emotional and may jump to conclusions without having all the facts. The Knight of Cups may also point to a relationship that has lost its creativity and has become mundane.

PAGE OF CUPS

The Page of Cups is a creative crow who finds inspiration practically everywhere she looks. The crow leans in and listens to a fish spin romantic tales of love and travels. This young, energetic bird delights in discovering new ideas and experiences, especially if they seem unconventional. Her vision of the world is almost childlike; full of play and wonder. The Page of Cups appears to you as a reminder that dreams can often provide the answers or inspiration we seek. Stay open-minded because alternative solutions may be found from a different and creative perspective.

Although upright this card celebrates the inner child, reversed, you or someone you know may be lacking maturity when confronted by a problem. An unwelcome situation may be the result of substance abuse or low emotional intelligence. You may also have unrealistic expectations that prevent you from finishing a project.

TEN OF CUPS

The happy couple sits on a budding branch of a cherry blossom tree watching their fledglings resting comfortably in their nest. The setting is one of peace and contentment. The couple achieved their dreams as each new day brings with it a feeling of love and fulfillment. The Ten of Cups denotes a time of utmost joy. Another message of this card may also be a romantic relationship is forming, one that could result in a lifelong love affair. Take a moment to bask in the positive energy the Ten of Cups offers. Good luck will soon enter your home.

Reversed, the Ten of Cups warns that you may be feeling disconnected or unable to spend quality time with those you love. This card can serve as a reminder to take time to reflect on the ways that you can create a more harmonious life with those around you.

NINE OF CUPS

The proud crow stands atop all the riches he has been able to collect. Because he actively went after each desire, the positive energy of the universe conspired with him to ensure the fulfillment of his wishes. His mission now complete, he can enjoy a life that meets all his needs and then some. He stands there feeling a bit superior but also incredibly grateful for his life of leisure and comfort. When the Nine of Cups appears, be ready to accept all of the abundance and joy of a wish fulfilled; you've earned it.

In contrast, the Nine of Cups reversed suggests that you expect the world to hand you your desires without putting in the work. As a result, you are only focusing on lack, and because of this you are finding it difficult to manifest the thing you want most.

EIGHT OF CUPS

The crow stands on the riverbank, her back to the gold cups that symbolize material wealth and possessions. She is ready to fly off and leave it all behind. The moon represents her shadow self and her true nature, one she tries to suppress but cannot deny. The Eight of Cups asks that you look inward and discover what it is you want from your life, what is important to you. This card suggests that although it will take considerable strength to let go and walk away, it may be necessary to achieve true happiness.

The reversed card indicates that although on the surface you want to build upon your spiritual self and move beyond materialism, the fear of losing out is preventing you from making a decision. As a result, you have become stagnant in your growth.

SEVEN OF CUPS

The crow rests as she dreams of all the things she wants. Some of her dreams lead to love and victory; others may result in loss or deception. Because she has created so many choices, she is finding it hard to commit to a decision, and as a result, she is stuck in place. The Seven of Cups advises you to step back and weigh all your options. Take the time to evaluate the pros and cons of each choice with an eye toward the realistic. It is okay to be a dreamer, but eventually, you will need to face reality.

Reversed, the Seven of Cups warns that you are spending every waking hour busying yourself to avoid facing reality. Because of this, you are unable to fully realize your dreams.

SIX OF CUPS

The crow returns to the place of his youth in search of finding his inner fledgling. He stands in a field of cups, filling his heart with healing memories of a time that was less complicated. If you have been feeling overburdened with day-to-day responsibilities, the Six of Cups brings the message to take a break and remember a moment in time when you felt free just to enjoy life. Whether it is a trip to your hometown or maybe a favorite vacation spot, it's time to recharge your spirit.

Reversed, the Six of Cups asks if you are clinging too much to the past and are unable to find joy in your present life.

FIVE OF CUPS

The crow of the Five of Cups stands on the riverbank consumed with loss and unable to find the path out of despair. Because his focus is directed only on what he has lost, he is unable to see the riches in his life. The Five of Cups suggests that you move away from a mindset of lack and look for areas in your life that are positive. The message of the Five of Cups: replace feelings of scarcity with gratitude.

When the Five of Cups appears reversed, it is a sign that you are learning from past losses and are ready to move forward. The ability to learn from past mistakes will enable you to see a path to acceptance.

FOUR OF CUPS

The crow in the tree pays no attention to the cup in the sky, nor has any interest in discovering the contents of the cups below. He sits detached from his community, unmotivated to do much of anything, and is bored by yet another shiny object. The Four of Cups speaks to a time of depression and the inability to find anything to be excited about. You may be in a time of self-imposed darkness whether it is from a disappointment or a bad relationship. The Four of Cups asks that you go inward and look for what brought you to this place of discontentment. It also may be a good time to take stock of all the things that have been going well, as that is the quickest way to raise low spirits.

When the Four of Cups appears reversed, it may indicate the hard work you have put in has paid off, and any hardship or difficulty will soon come to an end.

THREE OF CUPS

It's time to celebrate! The three crows happily play together and drink from cups overflowing with water. Food is abundant, and the warm sun creates a peaceful glow in the garden. Together, they are experiencing a joy that is achieved by the positive energy each crow brings to the yard. These crows want you to know that play is necessary and we all need to take the time to enjoy moments with friends and family.

Reversed, the Three of Cups may point to a time when you feel as though your voice isn't being heard, or you are feeling bullied by a group. Take it as a sign to reconnect with those faithful friends that may have drifted away.

TWO OF CUPS

The crows of the Two of Cups share the energy of water traveling between two cups and a divided heart. Between them is a caduceus symbolizing negotiation and partnership. The Two of Cups may represent a new romantic relationship. It may also foretell of a robust and confident business relationship. Together, the pair is balanced and equally satisfied, and share a unified vision. Similar to the Lovers, the Two of Cups denotes a karmic connection, although it does not necessarily mean a romantic one.

While upright the Two of Cups offers a harmonious partnership. Reversed, you are finding it challenging to agree with your partner. There may be a loss of respect or imbalance in power that has resulted in resentment.

ACE OF CUPS

The crow sits at the edge of the cup connecting with the profoundly intuitive energy of the water that is overflowing into five streams representing the five senses. Pink lotus flowers float in the water symbolizing purity and an awakened spirit. The Ace of Cups denotes the start of a beautiful, loving relationship and offers the opportunity for fulfillment in both the spiritual and physical realms. You are feeling drawn to those who are on a similar spiritual path as a way of creating more positive relationships.

When the Ace of Cups appears reversed, it may signal a time to curb your emotions. Doing so will enable you to see a situation, revealing the best path forward. It may also suggest that you have repressed your feelings for too long and have become cold or distant.

THE SUIT OF SWORDS

KEYWORDS:
Ideas, Logic, Disagreement, Knowledge, Thinking

ELEMENT: Air

KING OF SWORDS

The King of Swords is a strategic and logical crow. Using methodical steps and processes, he is the one who figures out positive solutions that benefit the group. His strength and poise set him apart from the flock. This bird is comfortable in the role of leader but is not power hungry. The energy of the King of Swords will bring a prudent and clear vision of success to the situation. The King may enter as a trusted advisor or may indicate that you are a source of reliable information that will benefit others.

Upright, the King of Swords is recognized

for his ability to handle situations with calming energy. Reversed, the King of Swords is an aggressive, manipulative, and greedy crow who cannot be anything more than a bully.

QUEEN OF SWORDS

The Queen of Swords is one tough bird. She is confident, independent and wise. Her quick wit, sharp intellect, and a clear vision of what the future should look like have garnered the respect of all those around her. Flying above her throne is a crow symbolizing her ability to see the big picture. When the Queen of Swords pays a visit, it may indicate a time when a stern, well-calculated and sensible solution is required. She may also appear as a mentor or teacher who inspires the best work from her students. The Queen of Swords card denotes a time when an impartial view is required to make the best decision.

When the Queen of Swords is reversed, she can be seen as a tyrant who is unapologetic, cold-hearted and short-tempered. She lets emotion cloud her judgment, and as a result, may risk losing respect and tarnishing her crown.

KNIGHT OF SWORDS

The Knight of Swords rushes into battle as the wind whips around him. He charges ahead, pushing past all those who get in his way. It is not malice or anger that propels him but pure momentum. The Knight of Swords brings youthful, enthusiastic energy to a job, which brings with it the inspiration to create a pathway to success. This card may indicate a project that you are excited about. There is swirling energy around you; you cannot be stopped! The Knight of Swords denotes a high potential and offers you the strength to complete the project, but it also brings a warning not to cut corners or make hasty decisions.

Reversed, the Knight of Swords cannot channel his energy to focus on a single project and as a result, attempts to go in too many different directions. If you are feeling scattered, look for ways to direct all that energy into a single purpose. The reversed Knight of Swords may also point to a person who brings a lot of energy but not the ideas to complete a project.

PAGE OF SWORDS

The young crow uses his strength and stamina to carry the sword through an intense energy storm. Along the way, he may have lost a few feathers, but it was a small price to pay for a chance at something more significant. The Page has found his stride and approaches the goal with a steady and relentless determination. The Page of Swords arrives with a message to throw caution to the wind, get out there and fly! The time is now to take action. The Page denotes movement, energy and communication, all of which are essential for embarking on a new adventure.

The Page of Swords reversed represents a person who talks a big game but doesn't have the experience to back it up. The card reversed may also warn of jumping in too hastily without proper research, and as a result, wasting energy.

TEN OF SWORDS

The defeated, broken crow lies on the ground at the bottom of a cliff surrounded by cold, barren rocks. Alone in his misery, this poor bird has been left for dead; impaled by ten swords. His ordeal is marked by the heaviness of betrayal. The Ten of Swords could indicate being back-stabbed, and may denote the end of a painful situation. If there is one positive aspect to this card, it is that the time of suffering will soon be over. This card asks you to let go and accept that an end is coming. By doing so you will find the strength to move on.

When reversed, the Ten of Swords may indicate that you are focusing only on the negative, looking for reasons to distrust. The warning here is: don't let fear of betrayal prevent you from living fully. If you direct too much attention toward this feeling, you risk manifesting your worries.

NINE OF SWORDS

Alone in her nest, the crow wakes from yet another nightmare. Scared to raise her head she cowers as the images of being trapped in a cage or caught in a deadly battle consume her thoughts. The Nine of Swords suggests that worry consumes you. There is an issue at hand that needs addressing, and inaction has manifested itself in the form of anxiety and fear. Your concern around this issue has the potential to manifest into the thing you fear most. The Nine of Swords is a reminder that negative thoughts can become facts.

The Nine of Swords reversed brings the message that you are getting worked up over nothing and you may risk losing sight of what is most important to you. Focus more of your energy on what is happening here and now and not on what may or may not occur in the future.

EIGHT OF SWORDS

The crow is caught in a cage of swords and wrapped in a long red ribbon that represents her limiting self-beliefs. She is a prisoner, powerless due to a lack of vision or inability to break free from her self-imposed cage. The Eight of Swords is a message to take back your power by looking at your situation from a different angle. The Eight of Swords denotes a challenge due to restrictions that appear to be overwhelming or beyond your capabilities. You have the power to overcome any problem. The Eight of Swords asks that you look inward to discover the potential within.

Reversed, the Eight of Swords indicates that a time of hardship is ending. As a result, you have learned lessons that will help you manage future challenges.

SEVEN OF SWORDS

The cunning, trickster crow is trying to fly away with a stash of shiny swords before the other crows can get them but there are too many for him to carry. Nonetheless, he is pleased with what he can take. The Seven of Swords denotes a person who is attempting to deceive you or is trying to get away with something unethical. If you are hoping to be able to trick or take advantage of a person, the Seven of Swords serves as a warning that your plans will fall through or you risk getting caught.

When reversed, the Seven of Swords marks a point in time where you are finding it difficult to take the next step because you may be feeling over-burdened. Now is the time to evaluate bad habits that hold you back.

SIX OF SWORDS

Through the snow, the crow makes a trip over choppy waters in pursuit of a better life. Along the way, he has lost a few feathers, but it is a sacrifice he made for a chance to rebuild and start over. The Six of Swords denotes a time that will require you to cut your losses and begin anew. This decision will not come easily, and there may be feelings of regret along the way. However, once the journey is complete, you will be able to recognize that the result was worth the sacrifice. Focusing on the new opportunity instead of the loss will help ease the transition.

When reversed, the Six of Swords indicates that you are reluctant and unprepared to commit to change. You may also be holding on to habits of the past that will not let you fully move on.

FIVE OF SWORDS

The victorious crow holds the swords of those he defeated. On the surface the victory may look positive, but in the end could lead to loneliness and despair. The Five of Swords denotes a hard-fought battle that you won, but the cost may end up being higher than expected. It could be a loss of friendship at the expense of being right or a conflict that will leave you feeling isolated.

Reversed, the Five of Swords indicates that you are tired of fighting and you have accepted that some gains are not worth the battle.

FOUR OF SWORDS

The crow appears to be dead, but he is going to a place of complete inner calm so that he can refortify his mind and body. He has encountered several challenges and there may still be more to come. But before facing any more tasks, he needs to take a wellness break. The Four of Swords is a reminder to take time out to recharge your spirit and your mind. Find a quiet place where you can freely travel inward and absorb the loving energy of your higher self. This card indicates you will be able to resolve your situation from a place of clarity and compassion.

Perhaps afraid of what the stillness might reveal, the Four of Swords reversed speaks to a person who is busying themselves with tasks to avoid the silence of their mind.

THREE OF SWORDS

The crow watches his partner fly away. The three swords puncturing the heart represent the pair of crows and the issue that resulted in the separation. The Three of Swords represents a time of sadness and loss. However, without sorrow we would never understand true happiness, and without loss, we would not appreciate all we have. There is no avoiding the sadness indicated by the Three of Swords, but this situation also offers a valuable life lesson, one that is essential for growth. This card asks that you take steps to learn how to heal your heart and your soul.

When this card is reversed, it is a sign that although much time has gone by, you are finding it difficult to let go of a painful situation. Or perhaps you are holding onto an old grudge. This is an excellent time to take inventory of your feelings and ask yourself which ones are preventing you from living or loving.

TWO OF SWORDS

The blindfolded crow balances herself on the blades of two swords. She calmly stays in place, unable to see the edges or where to safely hop to next. She is afraid of making a dangerous or painful mistake. The Two of Swords suggests you may find it difficult to make a significant decision because you feel you are unable to see the full picture or that there is valuable information that is being withheld. If you are feeling stuck, evaluate where the fear is coming from and look for the steps and information you need to proceed safely.

When the Two of Swords is reversed the problem with indecision is heightened. You are unable to find any clarity due to an overload of information, thus leaving you more confused and unable to figure out what is most relevant.

ACE OF SWORDS

The Ace of Swords brings dynamic raw energy, and for those who have the mental and physical strength, it offers a power that will quickly break through any barrier. The Ace of Swords card represents a time of ideas, problem solving and quick-mindedness. Whether you are arguing for a cause or answering questions during a job interview, you will feel prepared to articulate your position with passion and purpose.

The reversed Ace of Swords suggests that you are having a hard time completing a project because there is a lack of vision.

THE SUIT OF PENTACLES

KEYWORDS:
Money, Growth, Luxury,
Apprenticeship, Artistic

ELEMENT: Earth

KING OF PENTACLES

It would be hard for life to get any better for this King Crow. His savvy skills earned him an abundance of riches and he lives a most luxurious lifestyle. His heart is pure gold and with wings outstretched, he shares all that he has accumulated, from material possessions to his acquired knowledge. He is always ready to help those around him reach their potential. This King of Pentacles brings the message to live a life of determination, grace, and a good heart. In doing so, you too will find yourself living an abundant life.

When reversed, the King of Pentacles is overly extravagant and focuses too much on his outward wealth and status.

QUEEN OF PENTACLES

The Queen has come to you to offer loving energy. She is the quintessential mother, always at the ready to provide soul-soothing comfort that comes from her heart. Don't mistake her kindness and compassion for frailty; she is one tough bird who will do whatever it takes to ensure that those around her are well-cared for. The Queen of Pentacles brings security and balance to the situation, igniting powerful female energy that can handle it all. When this card comes to you, take a moment to bask in the love and security this merciful crow is offering you.

Of course, there is always the risk of going to extremes. Reversed, the Queen of Pentacles is the mother who smothers or pecks incessantly at her loved ones including anyone who crosses her path. She is over-bearing and controlling in all situations, from protecting the nest to foraging for food. It's her way, or no way. The energy at this time is fear-based and manipulative, and as a result, there is a lack of harmony.

KNIGHT OF PENTACLES

The Knight of Pentacles sits upon his workhorse ready to take on the next task. He has seen the Page's dream of focused visualization; and now, through hard work and determination, he will set the vision into motion as it enters the path to fruition. The Knight of Pentacles is slow moving and methodical. He is a hard worker who will ensure that each task is completed successfully before starting a new one. The Knight of Pentacles may appear as a co-worker or business partner who will keep his word and as a result become instrumental in ensuring the success of a project.

Reversed, the Knight of Pentacles risks becoming bored or stuck in the same job. He may also reflect a relationship that is not progressing or has become stagnant.

PAGE OF PENTACLES

In the abundant lush garden, the Page of Pentacles sits on a flowering branch. She allows the energy of blossoming life to enter her spirit as she gazes into the pentacle. Envisioning the path she wishes to travel, she holds in her mind's eye a clear vision for that which she wants to manifest. The Page of Pentacles' message is that to achieve the success you want, you will need to spend time developing a clear view and preparing for where the road may lead. With this skill you will be able to achieve your desire, and this is where the magic happens.

When reversed, the Page of Pentacles may manifest in the form of blockage. Take the Page of Pentacles in the reserved position as a warning; it's time to ask yourself if your enthusiasm has waned. Or, does your desire require more dedication than you are willing to give?

TEN OF PENTACLES

The Ten of Pentacles denotes a time of security and protection. The crows worked hard, paid their dues, and are now rewarded with a comfortable place to roost with plenty of room and food. The Ten of Pentacles brings assurance that your hard work and optimism can create a stable, secure future, one that will serve as a foundation to build your dreams.

Whereas the Ten of Pentacles upright is a clear sign that financial security is in your grasp, reversed this card may indicate a significant financial loss. It may also reveal a relationship that is just a passing fancy, however enjoyable at the moment.

NINE OF PENTACLES

The crow, in harmony with nature, sits upon a wolf as the sun casts a loving, warm light over the blossoming trees and abundant pile of coins. Unbothered by the bird, the wolf at peace represents a quietness of spirit and the ability to control one's emotions. In the distance is a dense green tree symbolizing a comfortable, stable home. The Nine of Pentacles may represent near completion of a goal or objective that will be successful once finished. It may also point to a life of wealth and comfort, both materially and emotionally.

Reversed, the Nine of Pentacles warns of financial loss because of poor decisions. You may have hit a roadblock or expect to maintain a higher standard of living without putting in the effort to achieve it.

EIGHT OF PENTACLES

The crow diligently and masterfully carves a pentacle in the coin. Away from the noise of the roost he is focused and determined to finish all eight coins to perfection. The Eight of Pentacles encourages you to further your education to master the skills that will enable you to become an expert in the area of your soul purpose. At this stage, it may be hard to recognize, but through hard work and dedication, you will find the success you seek.

While this is a card of perfecting your skill, reversed it may signal that it is your perfectionism that is standing in the way of your success. You may be focusing on a small detail while more important matters are left to chance. Step back and see the piece as part of a whole.

SEVEN OF PENTACLES

The crow rests after embarking on the difficult task of gathering a treasure trove of bright reflective coins that will adorn her nest and make a protective space for her fledglings. The Seven of Pentacles asks that you think about the long term when investing your time and energy. Although quick short-term gains may be had, in the end, they will not last. Only through hard work and planning will you discover lasting benefits from your work.

When the Seven of Pentacles appears reversed, it may be a sign that despite the amount of hard work and energy you are putting into a project, the result may not be what you expected. This is a time to trust your intuition and cut your losses if you are not satisfied with the rate of return your investment has yielded.

SIX OF PENTACLES

The generously charitable crow happily shares a fish since he has two and is not worried about finding more. Although he is a compassionate crow, he is not necessarily a philanthropist as he does expect some form of payback in the future. The Six of Pentacles denotes a time of receiving or offering help with strings attached.

Reversed, the giving and taking has become unbalanced. You may have given money to a friend who has taken advantage of your generosity or it is you who is not paying forward the help once received.

FIVE OF PENTACLES

The Five of Pentacles tells the story of two different groups of crows. The first group is comfortable and warm, roosting in the tree. The second group battles a headwind as they hop along the frozen ground unable to see that relief is just a short distance away. The crows on the ground may have lost everything, but they take comfort in the fact that they still have each other. This card serves as a reminder that even when all appears lost there are still opportunities if we look for them. It also serves as a reminder to feed your spirit by focusing less on materialism and more on relationships.

When reversed, the experience of lack and financial turmoil is ending. Now is an excellent time to take inventory of all the beautiful things that have entered your life and focus on gratitude.

FOUR OF PENTACLES

The crow of the Four of Pentacles has accumulated wealth and is financially secure. She has created a comfortable life. However, the fear of losing it all keeps her from enjoying her riches. Focused on feelings of scarcity and lack, this bird is so concerned with holding her possessions tightly that she is unable to fly. The Four of Pentacles denotes an inability to feel secure despite having accumulated wealth. This crow's warning: Obsessing on what you may lose will prevent you from experiencing joy from what you have.

Reversed, the Four of Pentacles suggests it is a fear of poverty that has created the inability to let go and enjoy the financial resources available to you.

THREE OF PENTACLES

The crafty crows worked together to build a structure enabling them to easily reach the cherries. The Three of Pentacles encourages you to continue developing the new skills needed for working with a group on a common goal. Do not give into fear or feel disheartened if progress is slow. It may be an indication that you need to bring in a little help in the form of a mentor, but nonetheless you will experience success.

The Three of Pentacles is a card of harmonious teamwork. Reversed, however, the team is not functioning well together because of too many egos involved. You may be feeling as though your ideas are not respected, and as a result, there is friction within the group. A change of work environment may be necessary to achieve harmony in your career.

TWO OF PENTACLES

Life offers infinite possibilities. The crow is in constant motion, juggling her day-to-day responsibilities with her goals and aspirations. It is only through devoting time to both that they remain in balance. The Two of Pentacles is a reminder to ensure that the small daily tasks are not dropped because doing so could jeopardize long-term goals. The Two of Pentacles asks that you take inventory of responsibilities to make sure that you are managing everything.

The reversed Two of Pentacles is a signal that you are at risk or have already lost focus and the result could be a loss of financial security. Make sure that you are up to date on bills and other obligations before you drop another ball.

ACE OF PENTACLES

The crow lands atop a large pentacle once concealed by clouds. This spot provides a clear view of all the riches available to her. Because her desires are no longer blocked, the bounty this world has to offer from material wealth to spiritual knowledge is all within her grasp. The Ace of Pentacles represents a time of clarity and the ability to manifest your desires. Stay focused; the Law of Attraction is working. Keep a fixed sight on what it is you want to achieve.

Although the Ace of Pentacles represents financial security and manifesting, when reversed, you may find a project or opportunity is lost. It may also indicate a setback after initial success with manifesting.

THE CROW TAROT SPREAD

Shuffle the deck and quiet your mind, allowing for a channel to open to your higher self. When you feel ready, pull a card from the center of the deck and place it face down on the table. Let your mind wander peacefully. When ready, pull seven more cards at random, placing them face down in the shape of the crow, in the order shown below.

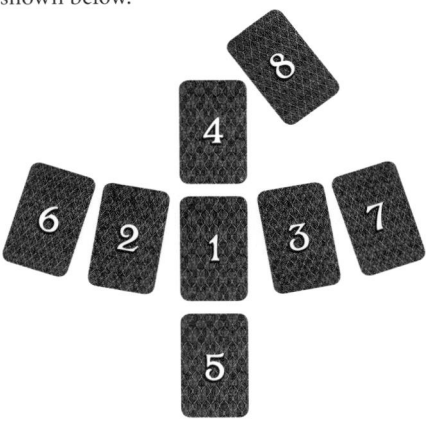

— Card # 1 —
HEART ENERGY / INNER SELF

This position represents an energy that is serving as a foundation. It may be one that is permanent and represents one's true nature or an energy that has taken hold of the heart due to life events. This card's energy operates in the background and is tied with the present energy.

— Card # 2 —
PRESENT ENERGY

This is the surrounding energy that creates the mood and creates the atmosphere for future events to emerge.

— Card # 3 —
ENERGY HOLDING YOU BACK OR HELPING YOU

This is the energy that may be supporting your goals or adding friction to the situation. Often the card that comes through in this position hints at your hopes and fears.

— Card # 4 —
HOPES / FEARS

This is the energy that lurks in your subconscious and at times can be a saboteur. It is the manifestation of hopes and fears.

— Card # 5 —
GROUNDING ENERGY / ADVICE

This is the energy that keeps you centered and connected to source energy at the present moment. This energy may come through as a positive card or one that carries a negative energy. A negative card in this position may signal that your grounding energy is counterproductive. This card advises you to resolve any negative habits or limiting beliefs.

— Card # 6 —
LESSON FROM THE PAST

This card is a past lesson or experience that serves as a reminder and offers advice for your current situation.

— Card # 7 —
EXTERNAL OPENINGS OR OBSTACLES

This is the energy that enters your personal atmosphere without your invitation. It may increase or alleviate friction.

— Card # 8 —
POSSIBLE FUTURE OR OUTCOME

This is the energy that will manifest as a result of action.

MJ CULLINANE
Artist and Author of Crow Tarot

———◆•◆———

Margaux Jones, aka MJ, is a Seattle-based artist, writer, mother, and lover of all things magical, especially crows. She attended Parson's School of Design, yet her unique technique of telling stories through digital collage is self-taught and has been her passion for over 10 years. Nature and its creatures are a familiar theme in MJ's work, however, having grown up south of Boston her collages are heavily influenced by the energy of the city. Her work often merges the two worlds. Her path into the world of Tarot was a beautiful accident that came out of a difficult time in her life. The process of creating *Crow Tarot* helped her rediscover her own wings, though at the time she didn't realize how life-changing the project would become. She simply fell in love with the process, the messages and the feeling each card evoked. The *Crow Tarot*, MJ's first published deck, has achieved a significant following and recognition with crow lovers and the tarot community. When MJ is not making art or writing for her *Crow Tarot* blog she is spending time with her daughter River, playing in nature, practicing magic, and finding new sources of inspiration.

For our complete line of tarot decks, books, meditation cards, oracle sets, and other inspirational products please visit our website:

www.usgamesinc.com

U.S. GAMES SYSTEMS, INC.
179 Ludlow Street
Stamford, CT 06902 USA
Phone: 203-353-8400
Order Desk: 800-544-2637
FAX: 203-353-8431